# BOLD and easy COLORiNG PaGes
# 5

## COLORiNG PaGes FOR aLL aGes

### aiSLiNG D'aRT
### and
### KaRa WaTSON

# welcome!

Inside this book, you'll find a variety of coloring pages... over 25 different designs. And, there are two copies of each design. So, whether you need a do-over, or just want to try some different colors... *you can!*

Go ahead, color them with colored pencils, markers, pens, or crayons... or combine different coloring methods!

Of course, these pages look great if you color them with solid colors.

Want more of a challenge? Many of these designs can be colored in gradients, from light to dark, or from warm to cool colors. (You'll find additional tips at the back of this book, including embellishment ideas.)

Of course, no matter how you color or which tools you use, these pages are designed to help you de-stress and *relax.* Find your calm with coloring!

Each design is printed on one side of the page. And, like most coloring books, it's smart to use a blank sheet of paper *beneath* the page you're coloring. That protects the *next* page from any ink bleed-through, or impressions from a pen or pencil point.

If you're looking for more coloring tips, visit ColoringGroup.com. There, you'll find information about other coloring books, and free coloring pages, too.

Kara and I hope you enjoy coloring in this book as much as we enjoyed creating it.

Right now, we're working on new coloring books.

If you have suggestions for our future coloring books, let use know. Use the Contact form at ColoringGroup.com or at Aisling's website, Aisling.net.

Cheerfully,
Aisling D'Art, with Kara Watson

P.S. If you enjoy this book, be sure to look for other books in the "Bold and Easy Coloring Pages" series.

And, for *different* styles of books, look for others Kara is creating, as well as Aisling's line of coloring books.

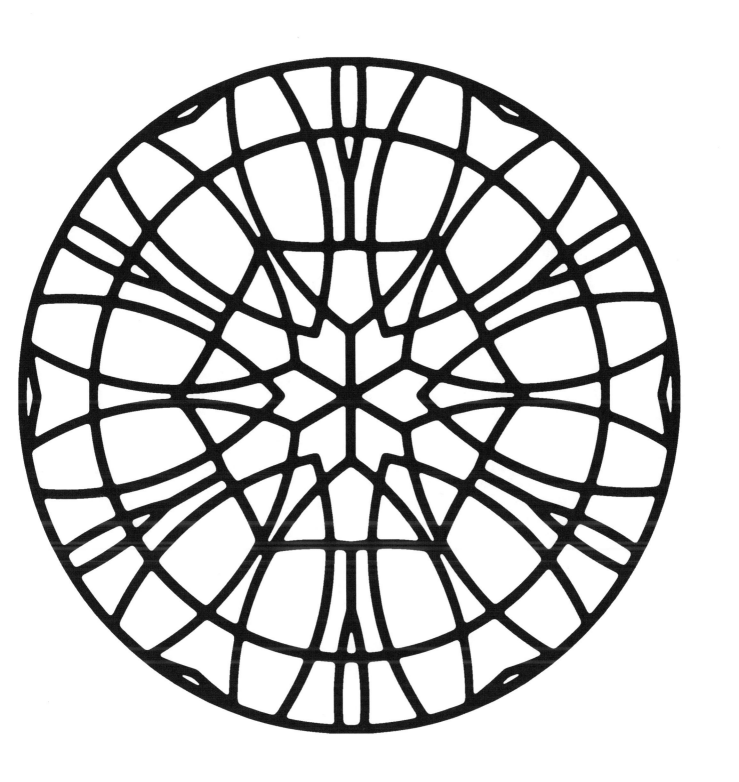

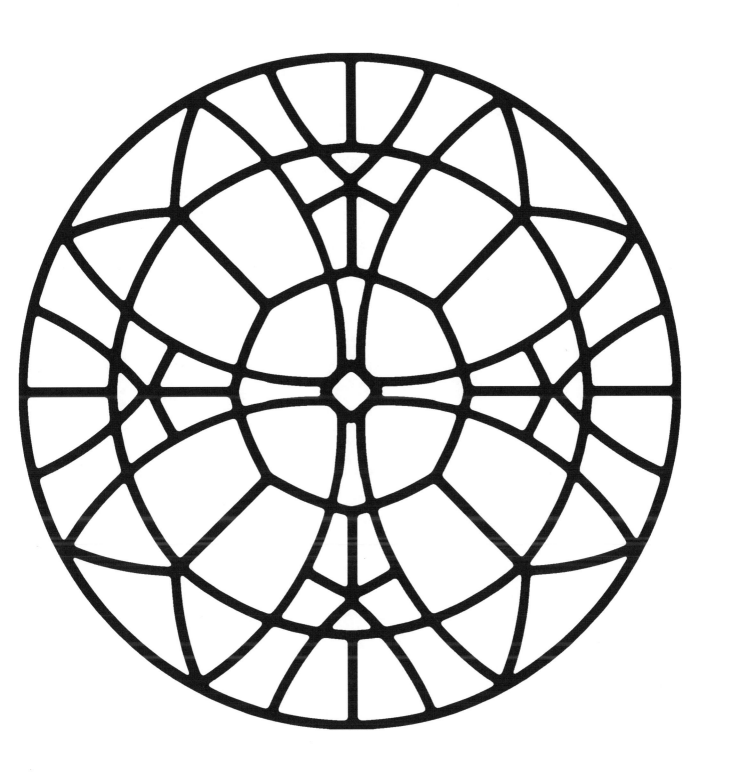

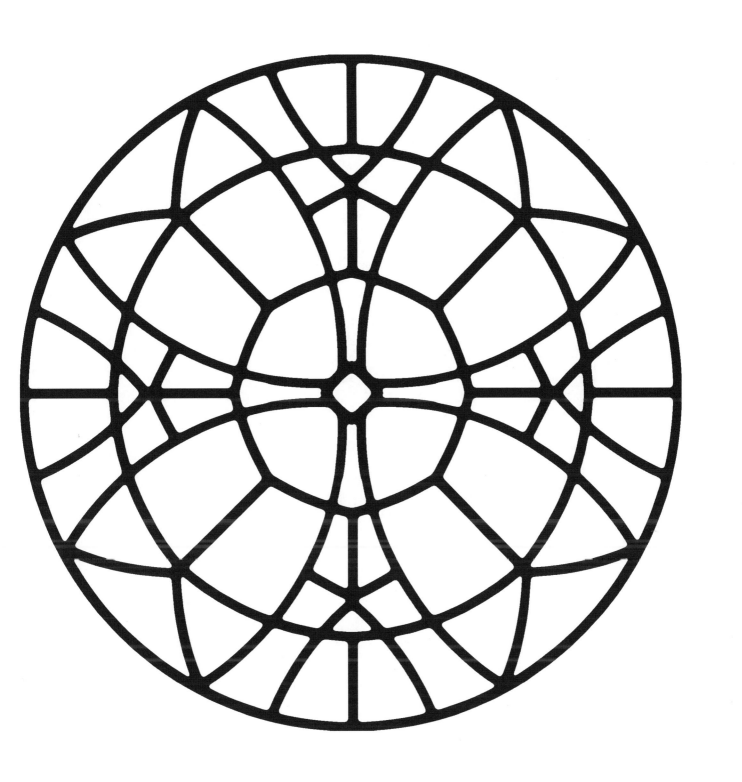

# Coloring Tips

Here are some ideas to get the most from your coloring books.

Remember Disney's "Frozen"? A single color (monochrome) can create a lovely, calming effect. Try different shades of blue, like an icy blue, a medium blue (or two or three), and a dark blue. Or, you may prefer to try different shades of red, purple, yellow, green, orange... or any color you like.

Crayon box colors can be fun, too. Try coloring with primary colors -- red, yellow, and blue -- for a refreshing, comfortable look. Or, try Mardi Gras colors like orange, purple, and green. (Just be sure to balance them with lots of white areas, unless you want a Halloween-ish look.)

While we're on the subject of white, it's okay to leave any area white. Or, you can fill any area with black, especially if it's tiny. In fact, you could color an entire page with black, white, and shades of grey. The effect can be dramatic!

If you're coloring for fun and relaxation, choose colors that make sense to you, even if they're offbeat... or *especially* if they're offbeat. For an Art Nouveau look, choose all muted colors. For a "psychedelic 60s" effect, choose brights and neons.

Want some extra flair? Doodle inside the design, or in the margins! You don't have to go "Zen" to add a personal touch to your coloring pages. Here are some ideas to use as fillers. Each square includes a few different doodles to inspire you. (You don't have to use them all.)

Basketweave          Ornaments          Concentric Circles          Arches

Spirals          Wavy Lines          Checkerboard          Decorated Hills

Note: Except for the Basket weave design, you don't need to sketch anything ahead of time. Go freehand! You can doodle with colored pencils or markers, or even a regular pen.

For more tips like these, plus free coloring page samples, visit ColoringGroup.com.

(Doodle art by Aisling D'Art, author of over a dozen coloring books for adults)

49482707R00072

Made in the USA
Middletown, DE
17 October 2017